The Greedy Dog and the Bone

An Aesop's Fable

Retold by Annette Smith
Illustrated by Julian Bruère

Once upon a time,
there was a little dog named Jip.

He was a greedy little dog.

Every day, Jip would run
across a field, over a bridge,
and through some trees,
until he came to a shop.

One morning,
a man at the shop gave Jip a bone.
It was a big meaty bone.

"This is the biggest bone
I have ever seen," said Jip to himself.
"I will take it home and hide it.
No one else can have this bone.
It is just for me."

So off he went, back through the trees.

Just as Jip was running
through the trees, he heard a noise.

"Oh no!" he said. "Someone is coming!
This bone belongs to me.
No one else can have it.
I will have to run even faster."

So Jip hurried on,
until he came to the bridge
over the river.

When Jip came
to the middle of the bridge,
he looked down.
To his surprise,
he saw another dog in the river.

The dog was holding a bone
in its mouth, too.

The bone was **enormous**!
It looked much bigger than Jip's bone.

Jip didn't know
that he was looking at himself.
The water was like a mirror.
There wasn't another dog
in the river at all.

"I must have that bone,"
said greedy Jip.
"It is much bigger than mine."

Jip wanted to get the bone
from the other dog.
So he jumped into the river.

But as he jumped,
he dropped his big meaty bone.

Jip splashed about in the water,
but he couldn't find the other dog.

And he couldn't find the other bone.

Jip's big meaty bone was gone, too.
It was right down at the bottom
of the deep river.

He could never go down there
to get it.
He had lost it forever!

Jip swam over to the bank.
He was wet and cold and hungry.

"I will never be greedy again,"
said Jip sadly.

He crawled out of the river
and went home.